Insects

Blake
EDUCATION
Better ways to learn

Insects

contents

Lexile® measure: 580L
For more information visit: www.Lexile.com

Go Facts
Insects
ISBN 978 1 86509 463 2

Copyright © 2002 Blake Publishing
Reprinted 2004, 2010, 2016
Lexile Copyright © 2013 MetaMetrics, Inc.

Published by Blake Education Pty Ltd
ABN 074 266 023
Locked Bag 2022
Glebe NSW 2037

Ph (02) 8585 4085
Fax (02) 8585 4058

Email: info@blake.com.au
Website: www.blake.com.au

Written by Katy Pike
Science Consultant: Dr. Max Moulds, Entomologist, Australian Museum
Design and layout by The Modern Art Production Group
Photos by Photodisc, Stockbyte, John Foxx, Corbis, Imagin, Artville and Corel
Printed by Green Giant Press

What is an Insect?

Insects are small animals with six legs and three body parts.

Insects have three main body parts. These three parts are the head, the **thorax** and the **abdomen**.

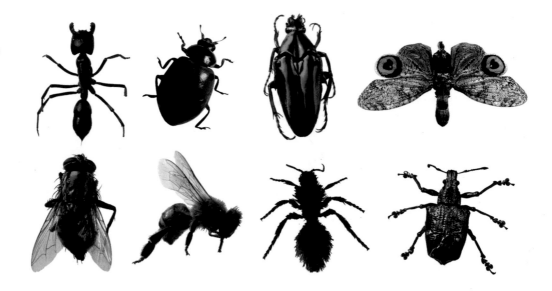

All insects have two **antennae**. They use their antennae for touch, taste and smell.

Insects don't have bones. They have a hard shell that protects their bodies. This hard shell is called an **exoskeleton**.

4

Some grasshoppers can fly.

Types of Insects

The insect world has a large number of species. There are more than 800 000 types of insects.

Many insects have wings. Insects fly to collect food and to escape from danger. Butterflies, beetles and bees can fly.

Some insects live together in large groups called **colonies**. Ants, bees, wasps and termites live in colonies.

Insects feed in two ways. Some insects bite and chew their food. Ants and caterpillars feed this way. Others suck their food up through a hollow tube. Butterflies, mosquitoes and flies feed this way.

Honeybees' wings beat 200 times per second.

A dragonfly can fly very fast.

Wasps chew their food, such as this plum.

Butterflies

Butterflies are insects with big wings. They have six legs and three main body parts.

antennae

wing

head

thorax

abdomen

The three main body parts of a butterfly are the head, the thorax and the abdomen. Butterflies also have wings. They use their colourful wings to fly and to attract mates.

Butterflies have two antennae. They use them to touch, taste and smell.

All butterflies begin life as caterpillars. The caterpillars change into butterflies. This change is called **metamorphosis**.

A birdwing butterfly gets ready to fly.

BIGGEST!

The wingspan of a birdwing butterfly is as big as an adult's pair of hands.

Insect	Number of species
butterflies	15 000
moths	120 000

9

Life Cycle of a Butterfly

How a butterfly grows from an egg to an adult.

1 Butterflies lay their eggs on a plant. Each egg hatches into a caterpillar.

2 The caterpillar eats some of the plant and grows quickly.

3 The caterpillar covers itself in a hard shell called a **chrysalis**. Inside the chrysalis its body changes.

4 The butterfly breaks out of the chrysalis.

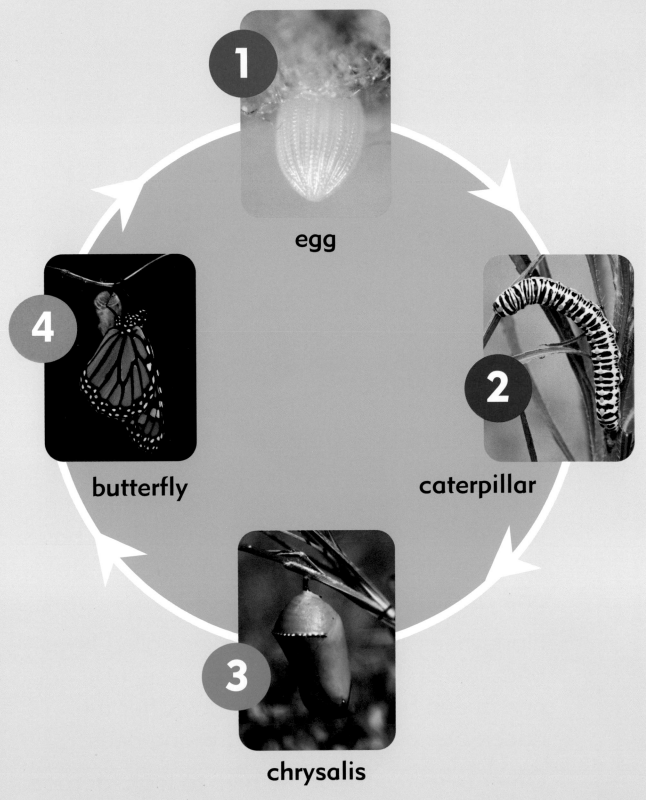

1 egg

2 caterpillar

3 chrysalis

4 butterfly

Bees

Bees are flying insects. They have six legs and three main body parts.

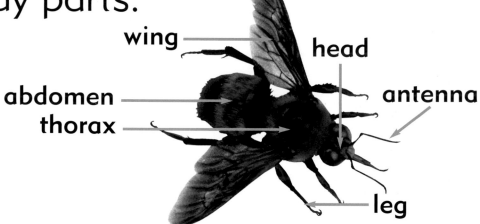

wing — head

abdomen —

thorax —

antenna

leg

A bee has a head, a thorax and an abdomen. Bees also have two pairs of wings. They have two antennae that they use to touch, taste and smell.

Honeybees live in large colonies called **hives**. Bees live and work in the hive. Every hive has one queen bee. Some bees look after the queen bee and the young, growing bees.

Other bees fly out of the hive to look for food. They collect **nectar** and pollen from flowers.

Honeybees work in the hive.

GO FACTS

DID YOU KNOW?

The queen bee can lay up to 1 500 eggs a day.

Insect	Number of species
honeybees	1 000
wasps	110 000

Life Cycle of a Bee

How a honeybee grows
from an egg to an adult.

1 The queen bee lays all the eggs. She lays each egg inside a **honeycomb** cell.

2 Each egg grows into a **larva**. Worker bees feed and care for the larva.

3 The larva grows into a **pupa**. The pupa changes into a bee.

4 The adult bee breaks out of the honeycomb. Growing from egg to adult takes about three weeks.

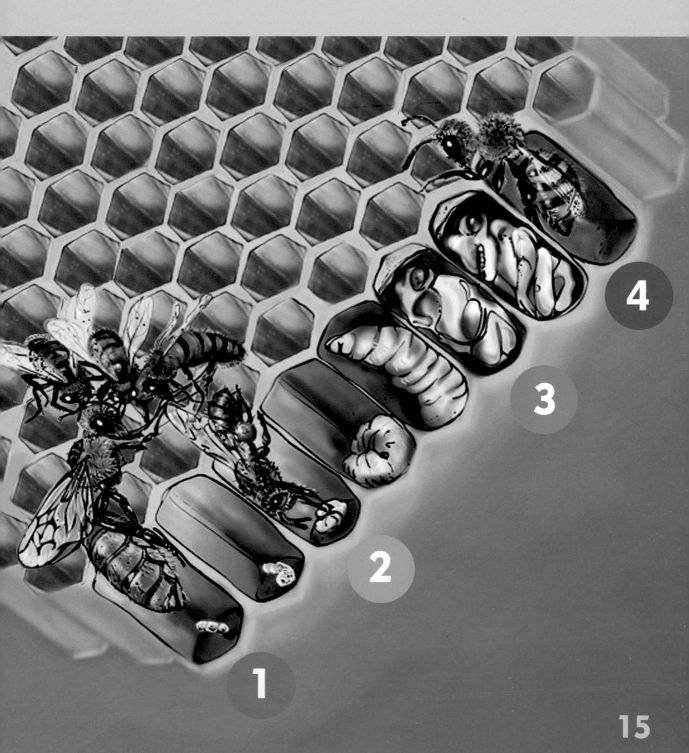

Ants are insects. They have six legs and three main body parts.

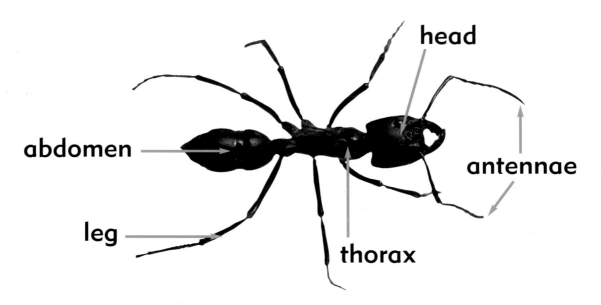

Ants have three main body parts. These three parts are the head, the thorax and the abdomen.

Ants have two antennae. They use them to touch, taste and smell.

Ants live in large colonies called nests. A nest has many rooms.

Ants carry eggs and larvae.

GO FACTS

DID YOU KNOW?

Leaf-cutter ants are farmers. They carry leaves back to their nest, chew them up and grow a fungus on them. All ants in the nest eat the fungus.

Insect	Number of species
ants	over 8 000

Life Cycle of an Ant

How an ant grows from an egg to an adult.

1 Every ant colony has a queen ant who lays all the eggs. Worker ants carry the eggs to other rooms in the nest.

2 A larva hatches out of each egg. Nurse ants feed and care for the larvae.

3 Each larva covers itself in a firm shell. It is now called a pupa.

4 After two or three weeks, the adult ants break out of their shells.

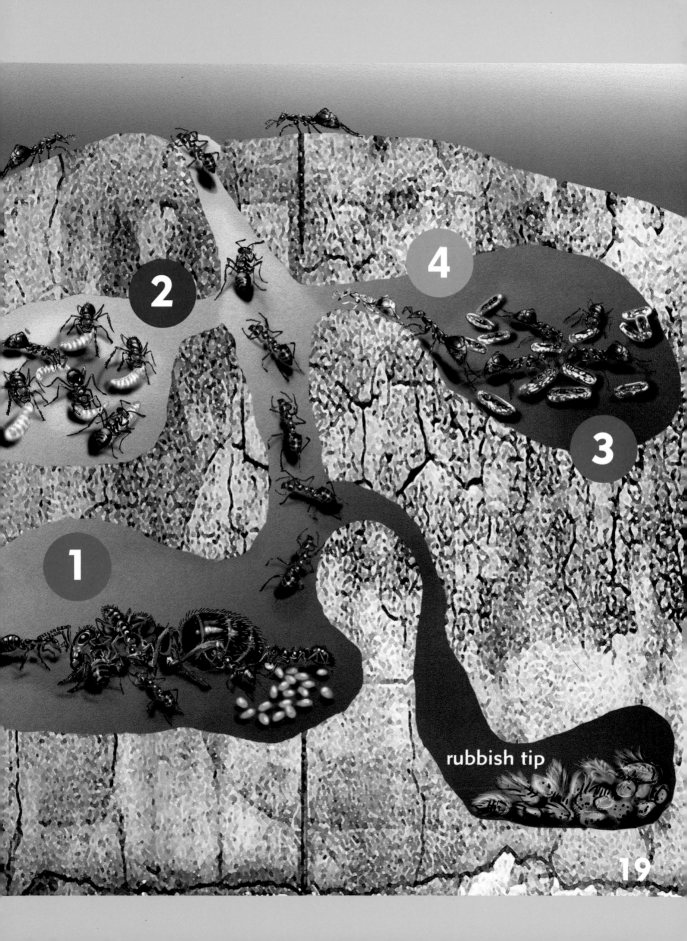

rubbish tip

Beetles

Beetles are insects. They have six legs and three main body parts.

head
antennae
thorax
abdomen
leg

The three main body parts of a beetle are the head, the thorax and the abdomen.

One pair of wings is hidden under hard outer wings. These outer wings form a hard shell over the beetle's body.

There are many different types of beetles. There are more beetles than any other insect. They live all over Earth, except in the oceans.

You can see two pairs of wings on this ladybird beetle.

GO FACTS

HEAVIEST!

The goliath beetle can weigh as much as three mice.

Insect	Number of species
beetles	over 300 000

	1	2	3	4
butterfly	egg	caterpillar	pupa	adult
ant	egg	larva	pupa	adult
bee	egg	larva	pupa	adult
beetle	egg	grub	pupa	adult

22

Glossary

abdomen	the last body part of an insect
antennae	the feelers on an insect's head for touch, taste and smell
chrysalis	the shell around a pupa
colony	a group of animals living together
exoskeleton	the skeleton on the outside of an insect's body
hive	a home for honeybees
honeycomb	wax rooms in a beehive
larva	a soft-bodied, wormlike, young insect
metamorphosis	the change from one form to another
nectar	a sweet food from plants that bees make into honey
pupa	an insect inside the chrysalis
thorax	the insect body part between the head and the abdomen

Index